The Galactic Council

Book 2

Front cover image courtesy of the Hubble space telescope.

www.imetatron.com

The time has come for Humanity to understand the mightiness of their being. The time has come for Mankind to grow up. The time has come for you to realize finally how powerful you are. That although your physical vessels originate on this planet that you have been seeded here as the seventh grand experiment on the Earth of Humanity. You are by far the most powerful mix so far and your capabilities expand much further than you could ever imagine. You are cosmic beings, able to be fuelled by light, by divine prana and as you access this more and more your vessels become energised, purified, transformed and lifted into your Adam Kadmon bodies. Purified and transformed into your upgraded selves. Your capabilities will increase and you will not feel shackled to those who would try to oppress you or believe in any of that oppression.

You are free, you are powerful, you are mighty divine beings, you are Avatars, you are ready to hear this message, you are Christ seed ready to flower and your light is powerful.

If you take the steps that we outline in this book. Your mental, emotional, physical and spiritual bodies increase in their power and you walk forward free of any need for the energy of anyone else for you will be walking Avatars of light. Fully synthesised. Your planet will transform and you will take your place as the greater guiding force of this planet. And all will look up to you for they will understand vibrationally that they can trust you. Your health and well-being will be an inspiration to all and your compassion will encompass all of mankind and all of the universe.

This is the final message that is needed to bring you into your full autonomy. Everything you do past this book will be playing in full understanding of your divinity. You are ready for Samadhi, you are ready for the full quotient of your divine bliss. And as you are reading this you are ready to take the steps to accomplish this.

The Galactic Council has been working towards this point in your evolution for many millennia and the events of the last century have served to further awaken you. The events since the turn of the century have multiplied and accelerated your growth to the point of awareness where you have reached critical mass. This book is in answer to that tipping point. It is the solution to the next step in your evolution. Embrace this message. Open up to the mightiness of yourself, the truth of your being. And your world will come into a utopia. Your vessels will be in bliss and your lives will be forever changed.

You have **the Clarion call** - heed it. You have been given **the healing book** - assimilate it. You have been given the **first mighty initiation** – allow it to sink into the very depth of your being and we will move on.

Read over these statement, fully assimilate them, and we shall begin.

Welcome to your future.

I am the Channel that Spirit used to bring this information down. It has been my great honour and privilege to be a part of this project.

I developed as a medium in a meditation circle years ago. I didn't know about ascension or any of the New Age stuff before I developed, but I always felt that there was something else in life that I should be doing.

Since learning how to channel, my life has become much better, and I am often astounded by the stuff that comes out. The process is simple - I go into a meditative state and I feel a great loving presence and hear a phrase repeated over and over. As soon as I hear the phrase, I let it repeat a few times so I know it is not just my inner dialogue, and then repeat it. After that I just keep on talking and sometimes can still be talking half an hour later.

This is all recorded and afterwards I transcribe it. This whole book was written this way, and it has been wonderful to feel the bliss that the high vibration brings. I have learned a lot from this whole process and my life is much better for it. I hope that reading this book brings you as much joy and understanding as it has done for me.

Best wishes,

Robbie Mackenzie

Warning!

We warn you before you begin that this process is not to be taken lightly. If you follow the steps that we outline to the letter, if you open your merkaba as outlined in the Clarion Call, if you do the downloads and upgrades from the healing book and the first initiation in the Galactic Council book 1 and you truly commit to the process, you will come into a place that you have never been before within your human vessel. But if you take these words lightly and you merely decide to stop eating, you can do great damage to your vessel, to your physical body and to your mind. We do not recommend that you stop eating fully until you taste the divine nectar flowing from your palate into your mouth. This is a process that every being who makes it to the next stage of your evolutionary process will come to. **All will fuel with the divine nectar**. This is how your species will travel the Galaxy, the Universe, and the Multiverse. This is what will fuel your bodies to the next stage of your longevity. Living hundreds of years and at the final process of the next step past this you will live thousands of years for you will constantly regenerate. This would not be possible without the divine flow from your pineal gland. We say to you if you have not prepared – to **STOP**, go back and prepare, prepare, prepare. Fully assimilate everything and come back ready to make the commitment to the future of yourself, your species, and your world. This is the most important evolutionary leap that you have made as humans since you learned to talk, since you learned to communicate, and this is a conscious evolutionary leap. Once you have made this leap, once you have crossed this bridge, once you have taken this step. And once you understand what it is to be fueled by divine nectar, you will never look back and you will see how simplistic your life was before this change. Be ready to draw a line in the sand between your old life the way it was and your new life the way it is ready to become.

Read this statement, re-read it, fully assimilate it, discern whether you are ready for it and if you are not, go back and do your work.

For those who are ready – let us begin.

We will begin by giving you the first initiation in the book. This is the second initiation overall. Everyone who is reading these books is positioned below a ship of light. As you do these initiations, the ship of light that you are going to be gifted is the one that is overhead at the time. Your connection is acclimatizing and resonating with the ship that you will be working with for this lifetime.

All who are in the room should stand up at this point.

Put your hands on your heart

You are now inside a beam of light that is beaming directly from your ship of light

Repeat the statement

"I surrender to the divine light. My will is thy will. Thy will be done"

Feel the power of this energy flowing through you.

This beam of light goes directly from your ship of light straight into Mother Earth. You are in the centre of it. When you come aboard your ship it will be this beam of light that brings you on board. You may now relax. You may feel very sedated after this initiation. Allow yourself to rest, relax and drink plenty of water. Allow it to sink into the very core of your being.

We have let this truth sink into your consciousness over many decades with the channeling of your science fiction series Star Trek. And when they beam on board, this is exactly how you will get on board. And although the ships can land and you can physically walk on board, it saves much time especially when you are in a position where you are in a built up area or you have to leave somewhere quickly.

As mankind escalates in its polarity and its density increases you will be free of this most of the time once you have acquired your ship. You will not have to participate within the dense three-dimensional illusion of fear, provocation, illusion and panic that will ensue at times. The more peaceful you are and the easier it is for you to get around, the better.

Mr Spock from Star Trek made a hand gesture popular for many decades that comes from a religion of light on the earth plane that has its origin on the star systems of Orion. To hold this hand mudra is to put blessings of peace upon another. It is to recognize duality of both involved in the greeting, the gesture. And once it has been made, in closing the fingers again is to understand the oneness of all beings. There are no coincidences dear ones. This has been spread throughout your culture for a reason. The teaching of this religion of light is for all the people on the Earth plane. No matter your familial religion. All gestures of peace raise the vibration of the planet and can help unify mankind.

Over the next forty-eight hours you will be seeing flashes of your column of light and you being inside it. Focus deeply upon this image in your third eye. Familiarize yourself with the feeling you have as the column of light embraces you. This is preparing you for your ship. The more you concentrate on your column of light, the harder it will be to hold onto any negativity. As you visualize this column of light you are being surrounded by Archangel Michael who is cutting the ties of all that does not benefit you on a vibrational level. Any that are holding onto you in a manipulative fashion and all thought forms that hinder you. This initiation is a true blessing on many different levels. We encourage you to picture it as often as you can over the next forty-eight hours. You will feel your being lifting up. And the more you allow the cutting of the ties with Archangel Michael, the lighter you will feel. These ties are being cut on every conceivable level. This beam of light grounds you into Mother Earth deeply into the core of the planet. And you will have glimpses of you bi-locating into your ship the more you allow this to embed into your consciousness.

This initiation is being overshadowed by the whole of the Galactic Council as each member gives a portion of their thought power into the emancipation of newbies. And you will feel the waves of benevolence come upon you. This is further helping to clear your pineal gland to bring your vessel into alignment with its divine purpose and joy. This initiation is a reliever of stress and it cloaks you in the light of comfort, detaching you more and more from the earthly realm. Readying you to participate in the affairs of the universe. The more often you think of this and put your hands on your heart, breath deeply and with every breath allow yourself to feel the comfort that is being put upon you, the better.

Your psychological addiction to food and your social interactions with food are very deeply ingrained upon your society. You use it as a way of communing socially, of meeting up in groups, tribes, in many different social settings around the dinner table. We do not say this is a bad thing, however as you move forward towards breatharianism and the divine nectar starts to flow in your pallet you will be freed up from the time spent in your daily lives preparing food, eating food, clearing away your table and cleaning your dishes. You do this three, sometimes four times a day depending upon your individual social structure. Part of the ease that is brought upon your transition going from vegetarian to raw vegan to liquidarian will prepare you for breatharianism in this way also. Your social interactions will be much more meaningful on a deeper level, not just surrounding the food that you eat. We understand how deeply ingrained it is upon your society and within your consciousness which is why we encourage you to transition through the different levels before you rely wholly, solely upon the divine nectar. But once you have made this transition you will never look back and you will realize the energy levels you have within your vessel when you do not have to process food will make you more productive in your daily lives than you have ever been. A great amount of your energy is used in digesting the food that you consume. Not only will that energy be freed up once you make the transition but the divine nectar in itself greatly energizes you, heals you and gives you all the nutrients that you could ever need. In order to break the chains from psychological and social addiction to food and to dining, we give you an upgrade.

This will help lessen the psychological effects within your being so there is no shock when you do all the social interactions that you did previously when the divine nectar starts to flow.

Relax

Come into prayer pose

Allow this upgrade

This will be very subtle within your vessel and will kick in once the divine nectar starts to flow.

We do not suggest that once the divine nectar starts to flow that you cannot eat, or you will not eat, or you should not eat. But the need for eating will not be there anymore. And you will find yourself much more comfortable within your vessel when you are aligned for the divine nectar. There will be many times where you will be called to social appearances, social interactions that you will want to participate in as you are divine catalysts for the world and your presence is very important. Therefore understand that this upgrade does not preclude you from dining. It merely helps you not have a shock within your system when you stop these activities in general on a daily basis.

The more and more you connect with your ships of light, the more familiar you will become with the controls. We encourage you to picture your beam of light daily. Allow yourself to be taken into your ship of light in your merkaba initially in order to energetically acclimatize before you are ready to physically beam on board. We call this the first wave of ascension as more and more within your physical interactions you will have the feeling of being two places at once and begin to recognize the difference in vibration you have now you have had this initiation. As you visualize this in your groups of three, seven and beyond there will be opportunities, especially in the larger groups for you to ascend on board larger ships, or mother ships together in group meditations.

We encourage this greatly for in your larger groups you will have greater opportunities to discuss the beings you meet that are stationed around the globe, helping your groups come together, energizing your groups and preparing you for your group ascension as well as your individual ascension into your personal ships of light.

Your understanding of galactic energy, of the cosmic flow is in its very infancy. You will make yourselves empty cups, ready to be filled up. You will experience a well being that cannot be experienced when you have any other vibration apart from the flow of divine nectar within your vessels. And as you begin to experience this, you will recognize just how primitive the way you have been living previously was. All ways of living are valid dear ones. But as you allow yourself to be fueled with cosmic energy, as you fuel yourself with the divine nectar and as you are filled up with the different strains of galactic beverage (Laughs) you will experience beautiful, clean, magnificent highs. For the essence from some star systems are purely, divinely intoxicating the way you experience your alcohol and your different forms of drugs, your caffeine, your different highs of choice, but you will much prefer the intergalactic cosmic tipple. Not only do these essences bring you to a heightened state of feeling nirvana but they also connect you into different forms of intelligence and different expanded experiences of bliss. The first experience of this you will have will be the divine nectar flowing from your pineal gland into your palate. With the clarity it gives you, the equanimity and balance within your vessel that you experience, you will wonder why you did not inquire about this before. This is only the beginning dear ones, there is much fun ahead of you. And as your humility with this process expands and you let go of attachment to your old ways of being you will be introduced more and more to the wonders of the multiverse.

As these concepts increase and become more widespread on the Earth. Be ready for opposition. For the more that taste of the divine nectar and come to rely less and less upon physical food. It will ultimately put your food industry out of business. It will become obsolete. The medicinal part of your pharmaceutical industry will become obsolete also.

Your farms that rear livestock and grow food will go out of business for lack of custom. And while this is still a long way off happening for the wider humanity, there will be opposition to these concepts the more widespread they become. Be prepared for this and stay in your zero point. Stay in your divine centre. For this opposition does not have to affect your vibration. And the more you take upon yourself the full embodiment of your magnificent selves, the less this will affect you in any way. Until the Earth is fully ascended this will be a consideration. And these people will fight tooth and nail to protect their income. Do not focus on this, focus instead on your bliss.

The Amartha wish to introduce you to their home planet. After you have become familiar with their part of the world and embrace their hospitality within the Earth. They will take you into their temples. At the door of their temples they have massive crystal skulls. And before you enter you will be asked to put your hands on these crystal skulls. As you put your hands on these crystal skulls you will fall into a deep, temporary meditation that will seem to last for a long time but will only actually last a few moments in your linear time. You will have an opportunity to do this in meditation before you meet the Amartha and many smaller skulls are being readied for you to meditate with. The Amartha are excited that they will finally get to meet you in person. And at last your story of Bigfoot will be explained.

The more you commit to this process, the easier and more organized your life will become. As you surrender to divine will it does not mean you have no will. It just means that the higher part of yourself that is much more organized and divine and for your higher good, for your betterment, the fruition of all your plans, your perceived success with your romance, with your education, with your exercise, with your diet and all things in your life become better. You become a better version of yourself. Expanding your mental awareness, expanding your heart most importantly. For your heart intelligence is your divine intelligence dear ones. It is your heart where you process the love. It is your heart where you experience the love. It is your heart chakra that is the bridge between heaven and earth. It is the centre place.

When you hear the saying 'The kingdom of God is within you' it is within your heart. This is the centre point of where the two halves of your merkaba take off, join together and expand in full awareness and you come into Samadhi. Into the expansion of yourself that is your divine God self, is the love, pure bliss, and the divine fire that engulfs you completely. In this place as you put your will over to the divine will, you become a walking extension of the Godhead. The upgraded version of your ego self, no longer dominated by your lower chakras. And it is this heart place where all good things will grow in your life. The more you cultivate this, the more you will see this reflected in the outside world. The more you open the heart, the more you become one with the divine heart of God that loves all things, that is all things and is the solution to all your perceived problems. When you are fully opened in this way you will be ready to take possession of your ships of light. Being in this place of deep heart wisdom is the requirement for the next stage of your evolution. In you opening to the flow of your divine nectar, you will be walking constantly in your higher self. Walking in the will of God. Embodying the peace that passes understanding. Living your mastery and having more fun than you could have ever pictured.

Hold firm to your resolve and your patience with this process, be easy with yourselves, be gentle with your progress and allow the energy to come upon you gradually. For this is the greatest transition that mankind has ever made. And we understand that it may be overwhelming within your vessels as you have not made such a grand evolutionary leap for thousands of years. As this is a conscious evolutionary leap it requires your conscious participation. You get to embrace and feel the transition on a very real, physical, personal level. The training wheels have been taken off dear ones. You are ready for this information. Ready to come into your power. This book works on many different levels, as does the first Galactic Council book. For those who are only ready to embrace these concepts on a meditational level that is as far as you will go and your lives will be made much better. Those who are ready to actually physically travel the universe and to board the ships, they will be taking a leap of faith. As you open up to the divine nectar and embrace this alternative way of fuelling, life will truly be magnificent and exciting.

And though after a year of helping your planet, physically you will be able to travel the universe. Most will still want to reside on this planet in the longer term to help your species evolve. There are those who will take on these concepts and help spread the word throughout humanity through discussion and even incredulity that this is a fantastic theory. But all three of these things are valid for your ascension is a gradual one. For those who have been waiting for the return of the Christ, those who have been already actively fasting, surrendering to the Christ heart with the principals of unconditional love through Jesus and the Holy Spirit are already prepared and have been waiting for a long time for this to happen. We encourage these ones who have been preparing for a long time to test these concepts out and to use 'Metatron, this is the Clarion Call' replacing the name of Metatron with the name of Jesus, to ask the Holy Spirit to guide you and to come into the Promised Land.

All the beings on the Earth are feeling this transition, are feeling the anticipation of the rapture and the tribulation. You only need to surrender to the Lord Jesus Christ and the kingdom of God that is within you in order to feel the power of what is happening right now. Those who have a different familial tradition, no matter which spiritual tradition, we encourage you to surrender to the deity you trust the most. For in so doing you will feel the unity of the Christ grid and all the masters embracing you in this next period of your emancipation.

The purer you become, the closer to the Godhead you approach, the stronger is the testing. Whatever needs worked out within your personal aura. Within your ego, within your mental, emotional, physical and spiritual bodies will be the focus for this testing. It will be very personal to you. We encourage you to focus on your beam of white light and your merkaba as these temptations increase. You will be brought into situations that will test your patience. That will test your Christ heart once you have pledged to integrate divine will as your own. Stand firm in your sacrifice. Open up to your bliss. Recognize this for the testing that it is and you will break through. The closer you are to the summit, the more surreal will seem the circumstance. Patience is the key to overcoming this. As it was said as you conquer patience you will conquer everything else also.

Once you master patience, you are truly a master. Cultivate your balance and equanimity and once the divine nectar starts to flow you will naturally be in balance and equanimity. And the peace that passes understanding will bring you into an ease that you have never known before. Embrace this peace.

As we review your progress there is always shifting sands. The tides ebb and flow and your consciousness raises and recedes and raises and recedes as you allow yourself to be taken. And it is a beautiful thing to go with the flow of the universal energy of your species and enjoy the transformation. But this point, this time is about you consciously taking control. And you making your will fixed pointed upon what it is that you desire, what it is you wish to manifest in your lives and how quickly it is that you want that to happen. These concepts we give you are not mere ideas. This is the reality of the universe. Joining consciously and physically with the Galactic Council. The more you let go of all incredulous thought and embrace this as a real possibility the sooner it will be that you can physically board our ships. And you can board your own ship of light.

The San Andreas Fault — is a point of great transformation.
So understand that everything is mathematically precise and everything is in divine timing for the bringing together of your whole globe in compassion for each other. Your natural urge is to pull together in times of crisis. Your natural urge is to help each other with great compassion and empathy. But there are those who are messing with the Earths natural timing merely for financial gain, for greed. Not caring about the wellbeing of the planet or the wellbeing of each other as a species. Only caring about the bottom line. This practice of fracking as you call it pollutes your water and is making the Earths mantle very volatile. More volatile than it is meant to be at this point. You are bringing your own demise upon you by allowing this and by not believing that you can do anything about it. You are beginning to awaken dear ones. Understand the power of your voice and you must also understand the power of your telepathic link with each other. For the more and more that you open up in meditation, the more and more that you raise your

Consciousness, the more and more that you join together. The more and more that you raise your vibration as a whole, the harder it will be for those who would oppress you and sell you out and sell your health and sell your well being for money to do harm to you. For you will be able to change the weaker brainwaves when you focus on your mastery. Raise yourselves up dear ones. Do the downloads, do the upgrades, do the meditations, do the initiations, come into your power. Your power will empower all that come into your sphere, all that come into your aura. For it is these things that are the abomination! And when you are allowing this, you are being as lemmings walking off a cliff. Do not be lemmings. Do not allow the suicide of your species. Do not allow yourself to go to war. Do not do the bidding of those whose only concern is money. Whose only concern is that of the few. You are a beautiful, divine species. We love you greatly; we have great compassion for you. We wish you to stand up, we wish you to come into your magnificence but we cannot do this for you dear ones. We can only guide you, we can only love you, we can only show you the path but you must tread the path yourselves.

The more you open up to your ships of light, the easier it will be for you to maneuver out of the places that are being destroyed, that are being tampered with. Now is the time to start this process. Now is the time to realize the truth of these words and to put them into practice. We urge you, **practice, practice, practice** your merkabas, Do the downloads, do the upgrades, embrace the initiations, expand your mental awareness with the Annunaki. Come into your magnificence, into your joy, into your laughter, and into your fun. You will still be aware of what is happening and you will have more compassion for those who are sleeping. Those who are still caught up in negative programming, negative hypnotism. And you will become divine catalysts to free all. Now is the time.

You will discover the remains of buried Amarthan bodies in Yellowstone National Park. The Amarthans were coming here for a long time and were using this place as a portal for many years, however, the site has now become too volatile and a lot of the access points have been merged into the Earth. Making it impossible for them to pass through in this place. The Amarthans asked us to add this fact into the book.

They are currently working with the channel of this book, with his guides for him to do a book exclusively with the Amartha. They have also asked that we put this part into the book.

Many different frequency modification tools that are given to you with different healing modalities, different traditions, meditation, types of prayer and different types of understanding of a spiritual nature are all very important right now. We encourage you to chase what it is that resonates with you but to practice it with all your might. For right now as the polarity increases it does not matter what you do, it is more important that you do *something*. We recommend that you open your merkaba, doing the healing downloads, opening to the upgrades and the initiations as these are the most powerful form of transformation on the planet, in connection with fasting, with exercise, yoga, and with deep breath pranayama in connection to the Annunaki, but no matter what you do, do **something**, raise your vibration. For there is in effect what is becoming two Earths. It is what people discuss when they talk about moving into the fifth dimension. Although there will still be one physical planet. There will be two very definite points - those who have raised their vibration and those who have not. There will be many who naturally raise their vibration within your normal traditions and there will be many who seem to not even be raising their vibration but are just there as divine catalysts. They will help you move forward through the trials that you need in order to come to the ring pass not and ascend to fifth dimensional living, thinking, fifth dimensional frequency. So understand that everybody is part of this puzzle. Although there are many who will stay in three-dimensional density and will be engulfed in pain and negativity. Everything is perfect dear ones. As you are reading this, in lifetimes before you have been at the point on a different planet that has ascended. And you have been one of the ones who have not gone into the fifth dimensional frequency. So understand that all that have to go through what is described in your prophecy as the gnashing of teeth and the painful great and terrible day of the Lord have to go through this for their soul progress. And at some point in your linear future they will ascend on a different world when they are ready. There is no judgment, and whilst we have compassion for all, you must detach yourself from attachment to those who are not prepared to heed the signs of their own soul. Or their warnings, whichever way you want to quantify what is happening just now. But this is happening on your Earth plane. Let go dear ones, set them free. Come out of your chrysalis and emerge as the butterfly, fly and show all the magnificence of your wings. Do not hold onto that negativity of the three-dimensional world for a moment. Work on your own ascension, your own impeccability, your own choices, your own meditation, your own prayer and your own love. The only thing you should focus on of the three dimensional world is to send them love. Pure unconditional love will help detach you, move you forward and help them dive into the lessons that they need for their soul. Every lesson, every point of pain, every death, every point of fear that they experience will help them further down the line when they are ready to come out of their chrysalis and emerge as butterflies. But a caterpillar cannot go into a chrysalis until it is ready for its metamorphosis. As you are reading this you are already in metamorphosis dear ones. We are excited to witness your transforming experience.

The more powerfully the cosmic energy comes through you, the more important it is to anchor it in fully, so that it becomes permanent. As you do this process it is very important that you do not have any animal products in your vessel. This is a twenty-one day process and will anchor the light fully into your physical, mental, emotional and spiritual vessels. This is the process of fully building your light-body. It is a twenty-one day process for each of the days concentrates on anchoring the light fully into each one of your chakras. Beginning at your base chakra. Moving up to your crown chakra for three weeks. For the first week if you have not already done so we recommend raw veganism or if you have moved on to a liquidarian diet for you to be juicing in this time. If you start this process as a raw vegan after seven days we recommend you half your intake for the second week and for the third week to be on liquids. Moving towards the final three days past the heart chakra day you will have sufficient cosmic energy to complete the process as the divine nectar flows through you. If you get to the final three days in the process and the divine nectar is not flowing we recommend you continue with liquidarianism and deepening your prayer and meditation.

These twenty-one days will focus your mental body on letting go of all preconceived notions and take you into a place of open mindedness about the process that frees you from the shackles of conventional thought. As you are released from the binding mental energy your power multiplies and you allow the flow to come through you more and more. This psychological change has a knock on effect on your emotional body. Freeing your emotions from all earthly negativity and binding agents. Bringing you into a full place of detachment and your spiritual body opening fully. As the flow of this energy magnifies, you come into the passion of the Christ, which frees you from all body attachment and completes the second initiation of the surrender to divine will. As you go through the process of the sacrifice and crucifixion of the physical body. For as Christ sacrificed his body for mankind it was to show his great love, compassion and harmlessness. And to raise up on a cross all that needs changed within the psychological judgment of mankind - **of anyone.**

As you go through this next initiation –

Stand with your arms at your side. In the position of the Crucifixion.

Picture yourself as Jesus on the cross.

Hold this pose!

When you feel the pain in your arms as you hold your arms out to the side. Repeat these words.

"I accept my part in the crucifixion of Christ. I feel the pain of his wounds. I am washed clean in the blood of the Lamb. Forgive them Father. They know not what they do"

Feel yourself being cleansed, purified and transformed.

When you feel you can hold the pose no longer, allow your arms to drop to the side.

Have a seat.

Visualize your column of light going up to your ship of light.

Those of you who are not of a Christian tradition do not have to repeat any of the statements. We do not recommend that you do anything that is not in line with your personal ideology. However. It is important that you hold the pose and feel the energy of the initiation. All who go through this initiation will feel the power of this in their lives immediately. And your lives will never be the same again.

By joining with Christ in this initiatory sacrifice and surrendering your vessel to divine will, you bring yourself to the point ready to **love all and serve all**. For those who lose their lives shall gain their lives. Those who let go of all shall inherit all. This is one of the necessary stages of initiation for you to go through which brings you to the centre point and brings you back into the divine template of the Adam Kadmon. For in the crucifixion, the " I ", the individual self, the ego, the separate personality self is crossed out. You merge in oneness with the Father. You forgive all for all past transgressions. You forgive yourself and walk into your mastery. Recognizing the purity of your divine essence. This is having the deepest impact on your four-body system. And will transform you into the next point of your consciousness – your super-consciousness, able to embody cosmic energy fully, able to ascend. For it was only after Jesus, who embodied the Christ, was crucified, that he was able to ascend. All the things he did, you too can do. For you are Christ seed. All you need to do is allow yourself to flower and be raised up. Past the point of the ring pass not in divine purity. Sacrificing all your lower selves, your lower chakras, coming into balance in the centre, your merkaba opening and you being fully emancipated upon your divine path.

This may seem very intense but if you fully surrender your will to the divine will it is a beautiful purified experience and will fully bring in the peace that passes understanding and lock your four body system into your divine mastery. We do not ask for half measures. We ask for everything. And in fully surrendering everything, everything you will gain. Once you have fully gone through this initiation you will have crucified all fear. You will have crucified all lack of faith - for the divine zero point, God, the Holy Spirit and for yourself, in yourself. After this crucifixion you are truly born again and your divine mission will be fully laid before you.

Earth, Air, Fire and Water. The four cardinal points of the cross, with you as the fifth element in the centre opens you up past this last initiation to the truth of your perfected self and the readiness to board your ships of light. The excitement is building and the more of you that do this initiation the higher the vibration around you will raise. After you have gone through this initiation all that come into contact with you will be deeply affected on a heart level. Stay in your centre dear ones for this will increase the polarity in many beings around you. All you can do is stay in your centre, stay calm and project love. It is not your responsibility to work out anyone else's karma or lessons of evolution. All are having their own journey. The only work you ever have to do is upon yourself and that that you are inspired to help with but always in love with detachment to the outcome. For it is not your place to take away someone's karmic lessons. You will only hinder their progress if you do this and delay their own transformation. Past this point you are an embodiment of the Holy Spirit. Perfect in your intention with transformation in your aura, you are a divine catalyst and although that catalyst may sometimes appear negative it is always positive for it is fuelled by divine intelligence. As you are reading this you have learned all the karmic lessons you have needed to learn in this lifetime to bring you to this point of transformation. If you had not you would not be a part of this. When you recognize the power of the energy that is being infused into this book, the first Galactic Council book, the Clarion Call and the Healing Book, you will fully assimilate them all and help spread the word to those who are ready to hear this truth. We encourage you to ponder these statements.

We are very well aware of the stage that you are reaching of the excitement and inspiration once you have overcome the fear and the cognitive dissonance associated with the fact that you are becoming ready to be a Galactic race of beings. This excitement, this joy will unleash massive amounts of energy within your vessels. We wish you to be ready and prepared for this, as this becomes a reality more and more in your day-to-day experience. The timing of all of this has been orchestrated to perfection for each individual soul that is on the Earth plane. For the ones that will not make it in this batch of your evolution and for the ones that will. There is nothing ever lost dear ones, and although physical vessels are ephemeral. The soul is eternal and the lessons continue past each incarnation. You are the God force and as you are becoming aware of this you are the ones who will ascend in this batch of your species. This excitement in itself in the unleashing of tremendous energy will expand your four-body system. The expansion of synchronicity and Goosebumps within your day-to-day experience as you recognize what is really happening will facilitate you to follow the inspiration and discard the energy that is trying to limit and inhibit you. There are always two paths dear ones. There is always a choice to lower or raise your vibration, the choice is always yours but it is time to walk into your magnificence. Time to let go of anything that inhibits you. All thought forms that do not allow your brilliance must be discarded now for you to raise everybody else up.

The individual merkabas or diamond lights as Metatron puts it, that are embedded in your chakras are being activated now. All points of your energy system are being activated upon the Kabbalistic tree of life.

Come into prayer pose.

The divine symbols are being downloaded for each chakra now.

The five trees of life are being activated within your full tree of life in your energy system.

This expansion will anchor you fully into your Adam Kadmon body.

And all points of the physical universe are yours to explore within your merkaba.

Earth, Air, Fire and Water with you in the middle.

You are free of all obligations and oaths, pledges and promises that are not in line with divine will.

This is the most Holy of detachments. Breaking the bonds to everyone and everything that would bind. All spells, incantations and words that would entrap you in your present, past and future self and bringing you into the pure zero point and the collapsing of all time into only this moment. From this point you can ascend and descend to any point within the game of life through the tree of life within your merkaba. Exploring all points, all people, all connections, all times and all projections of the one. Linear time is no longer relevant within this space.

This is being embedded and opened up within your consciousness so that you intuitively know how to use this part of your merkaba to divinely access the Holy words, sounds and visions that will empower you fully as a divine Avatar of synthesis.

Past this point you access your super consciousness.

And you access the power to create consciously, deliberately and omnipotently in your experience within this place. Your omnipresence within the zero point can only be accessed through this upgrade. This is the final freedom dear ones - the access to your oneness.

Once you come back into your body consciousness after this upgrade, allow yourself time to relax into this change.

We encourage you to come back to this place every day for at least five or ten minutes. The more you access this state of divine oneness, the more your conscious, individualized self will be transformed and the easier everything in your life will become.

You are the light of the world - beacons of hope for all humanity. Ready to shine your light for all to see. You have hidden your light for long enough. It is time to shine. Time to come into the fullness of your capabilities. Time to come into the fullness of your joy. Actualizing everything. You do not have to try too hard to excel within humanity in its current state of lethargy and sluggishness. This is not your fault. This has been engineered for you to believe in your lack of capabilities. To put those on a pedestal who you would worship instead of recognizing what they told you that the things that they do, you too can do. It is time to completely activate your light bodies, completely open up your merkabas. Transcend all different stages on the tree of life. Fully activating the Keta. Fully activating your crown. Fully anchoring yourselves into Mother Earth. With this current fully emancipated, and your flow turned on, you will shine so brightly; you will beam like the Sun. And all who have nefarious plans, who are trapped in the darkness of their beings shall be illuminated.

The meaning of the sacrificial Lamb of God being crucified for the sins of all mankind has its place on one level of understanding of consciousness. This is valid - to be washed clean in the blood of the Lamb, purified and transformed. But this must be understood on the other levels also. For what was happening in those times is happening today. Yeshua, Jesus, being overshadowed and embodying the Christ fully, drove the moneychangers out of the temple, in divine righteous fire, righteous anger. For money was the God that was being worshipped and those who were corrupt could not stand in the presence of the Christ. Jesus paid this price once and for all, for all mankind to see. For he was raised up on a cross, innocent of all trumped up charges against him. And this enigma, this puzzle, this mystery, is coming to light now in order for you to transcend your lower selves. For you are transcending the age, you are coming into the age of Aquarius from the age of Pisces. And those who will take this initiation and open themselves up to be overshadowed and embody the Christ, challenge and overcome the God Mamon. Challenge and overcome the money God. The worship of materialism, transcend this completely. What Jesus accomplished in his bravery and sacrifice raised him up for all mankind to see. All mankind resonates with the Christ heart for all mankind is the Christ seed. The Christ is your future, every one of you, even those who would deny it. The meaning of those who would take up their cross and follow the Lord is being fulfilled in this moment as you transcend the Cross. You fully emancipate yourself through the ring pass not and you inherit the kingdom of God. Those who profess Christ as King but who would deny a meal to the poor, to the starving, to the homeless, are but hypocrites and not fit to walk the path yet, immature within their soul path journey upon this earth plane and misleading humanity. Any who sit on a gold throne while one child goes homeless, sit on a throne of lies and must make themselves fit to do the work they have been appointed for. For the anointing is at hand dear ones. And the anointing will take place not at the hands of Man, but from the hands of God, using the Holy Spirit. Overshadowing his divine servants that are here on the Earth plane now. All is coming into alignment, there is no mistake, all is being washed clean. All who read this be aware of the path you are treading. You are ready to come into your wholeness. The feast of the Lamb is upon you. All are being invited to the table. Not all will be prepared to pay the price, even though the price is free. You will understand and you will see, that all who partake of this meal shall share in the glory of the Kingdom being established on the Earth and mankind once and for all being free. While one suffers, all suffer. You are ready to love all and serve all. They who are last shall become first and they who think themselves first shall be shown the truth of their self. Prepare, prepare, prepare.

Your original divine template is what your Adam Kadmon body is. You are growing in awareness of this and you will feel as if you are expanding into greater and greater levels of yourself but it is really just becoming aware of what you already are. You all have this divine template dear ones. You were always going to come to this point as a species. You have been working forward through your design for many thousands of years in this batch of your evolution.

Becoming more and more aware of your four-body system and how it impacts upon your experience in life will make your experience more complete. Just as you exercise to make yourselves strong, sacrifice fattening foods to make yourself lean, you are being called within your four-body system, to sacrifice your lower self, to exercise compassion for yourself and for others. You are being squeezed and pressurized with the situations that seem very dramatic on your Earth right now. Although the plan to entrap and enslave, dominate and oppress mankind is there. This is you being squeezed as a species in order for you to become stronger and rise up. For it is this pressure that antagonizes the muscles that makes them strong, makes them powerful in the same way you are being squeezed in order for you to rise up into your power and open your merkaba, to make it a necessity for you to be fit in your four-body system. For the illuminati, those who would oppress mankind... **Are you!** This is a reflection of your consciousness, your collective consciousness on the Earth plane. You are giving yourselves this battle in order to bring yourselves to the next step of your awareness, the next step of your consciousness, the next step in your evolution. So have compassion for yourselves, but take the steps, the necessary steps, to rid yourselves of this paradigm. To transform the world into the utopia that you can have where all are cared for, all are nurtured and all are considered. The sacrifice of your lower self once you recognize how lean you become, how fit and active, how transformed, how healthy, how your vessels excel in your four-body system, how balanced you are within your emotional body, how powerful you are within your mental body and how at peace you are, will be no sacrifice at all for when you sacrifice that which does not serve you any more you will be serving yourself. And this transition will become much easier. Have compassion for all beings that are going through this same testing. For all is perfect dear ones and this divine drama is serving to open up your Buddhic selves. You are Buddha's, you are all Buddha's. You are either sleeping Buddha or awake Buddha. Those who are awake see there is no problem, for all is perfect, all is just a reflection of the mind, all is just a reflection of the consciousness. And when you allow yourself to fully awaken, all you experience is the bliss of the universe. The peace that comes from detachment from opinion, detachment from taking a stance, the natural flow that animates all good things that cannot hold onto guilt or pain or fear or worry. The recognition of yourself as the universe, for you are the universe, you are source. You are Christ, you are Buddha, you are Krishna. You are all things. This is your divine drama and all who are sleeping are embracing the divine drama in this game of hide and seek. And when they are ready to awaken they will. It is not your job to awaken anyone. It is only your job to fully awaken yourself and in awakening yourself you help the alarm go off for others. Your active participation is always upon yourself. With your constant and never ending improvement of yourself into greater and greater awakening states. And when you are fully awakened you fully embody the Adam Kadmon, your divine template. All four bodies pull together and you are a walking example of mankind's next stage of their evolution.

You are the light of the world and you are here to light the world up. You are ready to come out of hiding and shine as the beacons that will enlighten humanity. Letting go of all shackles of self imposed perceived restrictions through collective perceived wisdom. Open up to the wisdom of spirit. The truth and the power of the Holy Spirit and be ready to fly in your light bodies. Once you drop all restrictions, all mental thought forms, all emotional shackles, all physical inhibitions, all spiritual blocks to bliss, you will live in a fully open merkaba state and you will be untouchable by any thought form, any ego that would try to oppress you, In this place you can play fully once again as you did as a child. But your imagination now can manifest very rapidly in the physical and you must use this power wisely to love all, serve all, free all and transform this whole world. One being can do much, but 144,000 beings can transform the whole world very rapidly. Although this number is in reference to your D,N,A it is also in reference to the amount of souls ready to awaken fully to their mastery. Getting the hang of their light bodies, getting the hang of their mental, emotional, spiritual and physical bodies. Getting the hang of their merkabas. Downloading, upgrading, transforming, absorbing the initiations and creating the utopia that you are ready to experience.

This is the book of the Lamb and you are reading it.
Allow yourself to absorb this statement.

Each and every one of you that is reading this is ready to become all that the Christ is ushering you to be. To fulfill your destiny, to create, to walk the path ordained by God. To trust that it will open up in front of you, that all blocks will be taken away. This is the moment. The trumpet has sounded. You have been raised incorruptible. And you can only read these words if you have been chosen to do so. Shine your light dear ones. You are the light of the world. All is being accomplished through Christ. You are being lit up ready. You are free.

Each part of your journey is mathematically precise. But every single move is not predetermined. Every single move is determined upon the different level of vibration that you are emitting. You have great creative control over your experience. As you are at the level of vibration that is able to read this book, the understanding of your creative powers is about to expand greatly. For you cannot get this far in the book without your crown chakra having been opened. And your light-body having been activated. When you understand the power of your vibration at this level of creation you will give no second thought to the drama happening on the earth plane right now but instead embrace your creations of your artistry fully. For your lives are artworks. Whatever excites you dear ones, whatever lights you up. This is what your Holy mission is. It does not matter what that is, just that it excites you and from moment to moment that can change. Be mindful of what you take into your bodies. What you ingest. Be mindful of your thoughts. Which ones you allow yourself to imbibe from others. Be mindful of those patterns that block your bliss, block your fun. Or those beings you find yourself in the company of who inhibit your joy. Recognize that the block is only there when you allow it to be there. And understand that anything they say or do to inhibit your bliss, your joy, is their illusion and does not have to be a part of yours. Once you have embraced this concept fully you will embody it and they will not be able to block your joy or your bliss. Be mindful of all events that happen as illusions of your consciousness and embrace your power to transform them on an emotional level so that you approach them all with balance, which will facilitate you transforming them on all different levels. It is the way that you feel that will determine your reality, connected with your mental body. This is why we give you the bliss download in the healing book. You are ready for this. You are ready to walk forward on your mission.

You are an awakening force and you must stand in your power. You do not stand alone dear ones. You have all the forces of light behind you. When you stand in your own power you are the light, you are the love, you are the peace that will transform the whole world. This transformation is happening. More and more people are awakening every day. As you are reading this text, your many different lifetimes on this planet have been geared towards this time. Geared towards the emancipation of all. Many of you who are reading this have sacrificed yourselves in many lifetimes. Have been martyrs to the cause. Have been crucified. Have been stoned to death. Have been persecuted in many of your different lifetimes for the sake of Christ, for the sake of truth. This is a lifetime of emancipation; this is a lifetime of completely changing the paradigm on the Earth. And fully embodying your light, fully embodying the Christ. This is the lifetime of your reward. For it was said the dead shall be raised incorruptible. It was referring to the martyrs and the saints being reincarnated ready to join with the other beings of the army of light that are here to free this planet. Do not rest on your laurels - you have much to do. This lifetime is the greatest lifetime of joy and of transformation and all the sacrifice that you have made in the past will be rewarded fully. You are here to create the new Jerusalem, to free all mankind, to fully embody your light, to fully activate your light bodies. You are being anointed dear ones.

Sit in prayer pose.

Accept your anointing in purity.

Allow the Christ to open up your heart fully.

Feel the power as you accept your reward for all your service in lifetimes gone by.

Your feet are being washed clean.

All of your D,N,A is being opened up for this lifetimes mission of transformation.

The visions of John are being fulfilled.

You are ready for this.

Your revelation is upon you.

You have proved yourselves worthy for this work. Purified and emancipated.

Washed clean in the blood of the Savior.

Washed clean in the blood of the Lamb.

You are fit to put on your robes of purity now - Incorruptible and pure.

Stand and accept this blessing.

You are within your column of light now. Your ship of light is up above. Your higher self, with all the power of your past lives and service, is in your ship of light. And you are able to access this power at any time.

The power of God is upon you.

The fullness, the effulgence of Spirit will come in waves upon you now you are anointed. And more and more as these waves come upon you the more and more you will be empowered and the less and less you will be affected by anything that does not serve your divine mission.

There are powerful cosmic waves that are coming from your central sun that will help break down the negativity on the Earth plane. The more prepared you are the easier these will be and if you have followed instructions fully from the beginning, from the trumpet sound, from the Clarion Call. These waves will empower you and you will only feel bliss as you will have dealt with any issues you have needed to within your psyche, within your consciousness. Individual warriors of Christ have their own personal template. You are unique and yet with the Christ heart you are all the same - all one in divine synchronicity. It is this divine synchronicity that will completely change the world. It is acting within your own divine template, your own joy, and your own bliss. Following your highest excitement at all times. Embracing what is in front of you, no matter what that is, as divine will. For if it was not divine will it would not be happening. Recognize that what it is you have to do to transform whatever circumstance is in front of you is only ever to follow your highest excitement. When you are called to divine sacrifice, you are being purified, sanctified, transformed, and in your transfiguration you will be forever changed. The light of God will shine from your face. The passion of the Christ will beam out of your eyes. Which will dazzle. The sword of truth shall come from your mouth and you will cut away all falsehood with your words. The crown is being placed upon your head. You are being imprinted with the seal upon your aura. Ownership of the King of Kings, Lord of Lords, bought with the final blood sacrifice. Your interpretation of any Holy scripture will be complete. Your words will be infused with divinity and all that come into contact with you will be freed. Your Christ heart is opening now fully. You are the light of all the suns, all the universes, the whole multiverse. Your heart blazes with divine fire, burning away all resistance. This is the second destruction of the Earth through fire. You are vessels of divinity, of transcendence, of power. Your mastery is complete. All the gifts of the spirit will open up from this point onwards. Your actions will be pure. There is no need for words past this point. Simply absorb the waves as they come upon you. With each wave you become more and more powerful, more and more Christed, compassionate, peaceful, loving and kind. Fear cannot survive with the Christ heart. You are on a different level of existence now. You are the elders, the leaders of humanity.   **You are ready for this mission.**

When the demons come and come they will to try to corrupt you, your transformational power now will disarm them fully. For you are the cleansers of humanity now. Stand firm in your power. Embodying the Christ light. All previous bonds are broken. Anything that hinders your mission is gone. This fire burns in all directions. From your heart you are a walking fireball. This is not an earthly fire that burns upwards, needing oxygen. This is divine fire. Purifying, golden, devouring all that is not love in its path. This fire, now lit, will rage throughout the whole world until the task is complete. This fire will affect all. Where you are in the world is the perfect place for you to spread this fire. In your groups of three, seven and beyond within your congregation it will weed out the vipers that are there in the name of Christ. It will change all from hypocrisy back to the divine template. All that profess Christ but for only power will be burned up in the flame. For all who hold Holy positions only in name, it will do the same. This flame will burn always within yourselves. Burning away all hypocrisy, all duality, all negativity, constantly on guard from the schemes of your ego. The analogy of the Devil, Satan is overcome and you are given divine power. The power of your thought is all you need to send this fire. The fire, now lit, shall never burn out. You are the burning bush of God. Nothing can stand in this fire that is not Holy. Your transformation is complete. Feel the waves come upon you more and more.

When you are ready for the twenty-one day process, you must prepare beforehand. Take as many artificial additives out of your diet as possible. Caffeine, at least three days before the twenty one day process. For the seven days prior, we suggest raw veganism. Moving towards day one, where, for best results, you should begin a seven-day juice fast. Green leafy vegetable juice would be the best for this process. We suggest you document your progress. For the first seven days do yoga asanas, chanting the Gayatri mantra, praying and meditating, opening your merkaba and being very peaceful. For the second week we suggest you begin day eight with just water.

Day nine back to juicing.

Day ten a water fast alternately up to day fourteen.

On day fifteen and sixteen water fast.

Day seventeen juicing.

Eighteen and nineteen water.

Day twenty juice and on day twenty-one we suggest you take nothing at all.

On day twenty-one if you are ready. If you do the exercises that we lay down for you, you will begin to feel the nectar start to flow from your palate. **It will be one of the most profound moments that you have ever had within this incarnation.** Once the divine nectar is flowing there is no need for any other type of substance. Do not fool yourself into believing you are ready before you are. You are working with divine forces now and nothing will block this. All of the divine Holy forces are on your side. And whilst it is true that everything is a reflection of the oneness. Within this understanding of your Holy mission within this three-dimensional reality you are being given the keys to every lock. **These keys are not available to everyone.** You have to be at the point within your divinity where you are giving yourself over to the divine light, the divine oneness, to the will of God, the purity of the Christ and the transformational mission that you have been part of for many of your lifetimes. This will instill within you divine confidence and assurance that your mission will be successful. Everything will be successful when you unlock yourself with these keys. These are the divine keys of Enock, the keys of Metatron, the keys of David. The keys that unlock your Christhood fully and they are upon you now.

Day one - You unlock your base chakra with the first key. In unlocking your base chakra you are unlocking the divine powers that anchor you fully into Mother Earth. And lock up any issues that have hindered you in your past, never again to be unlocked. All issues of security and stability are transcended and your base chakra is unlocked in its fullest sense. Anchoring you into the fullest and most divine expression of your base chakra. This first key anchors you fully. Locks you into your divine mission with your physical expression. It transcends everything that needs transcended within this lifetime and locks you firmly into the tree of life. Opening up this understanding within you. Expanding your merkaba within Metatrons cube. Once these issues are locked they will be transcended and cannot be unlocked once again. And once the power of the base chakra is unlocked fully, your divine mission is in place and the building blocks of the tree of life can begin.

Sit in prayer position and repeat.

"I ask for the first key of Enock to unlock my base Chakra. And to lock all the issues that I have ever had in my base chakra within this incarnation. I am that I am. And so it is. Amen."

The second key of Enock will unlock your sacral chakra. Anchoring it fully into your base chakra. Unlocking the full potential of your sacral chakra. Balancing and aligning all the issues you have ever had within this incarnation. Locking in your divine tantric energy within your four-body system in full integrity and impeccability. And locking up all the issues you have ever had within this incarnation.

Sit in prayer position and repeat.

"I ask for the second key of Enock to unlock the potential of my sacral chakra. And to lock away all the issues that I have ever had with my sacral chakra. I am that I am. And so it is. Amen."

The third key of Enock unlocks your solar plexus and locks your solar plexus fully into your sacral chakra. Unlocking the full potential of your power base. Locking it fully into your sacral chakra and locking it fully into your heart chakra. As it locks in your power and potential it opens up all your capabilities and locks away all the issues that you have ever had within your solar plexus chakra.

Sit in prayer position and repeat.

"I ask for the third key of Enock to unlock all the potential of my solar plexus. And to lock away all the issues that I have ever had with my solar plexus. I am that I am. And so it is. Amen."

The fourth key of Enock opens up the full potential of your heart chakra. Locks it fully into your solar plexus and your throat chakra. Locks it fully into the Christ grid and Mother Earth. Anchors your heart chakra as the central point of all things within creation. The key of Enock that unlocks your heart chakra unlocks the kingdom of God within you. This is the most powerful key of Enock there is. Unlocks your divinity fully. Unlocks the full potential of your heart. And locks away all issues that you have ever had with your heart chakra.

Sit in prayer position and repeat.

"I ask for the fourth key of Enock to unlock my heart chakra fully. And to lock away all issues that I have ever had with my heart chakra. I am that I am. And so it is. Amen."

The fifth key of Enock unlocks your throat chakra fully. Unleashes the divine potential within your words, your impeccability within your statements. Unlocks the divine nectar, the divine poetry within your speech. The kindness and the mastery and locks away all harshness, vitriol, negativity and all past issues that you have ever had with your throat chakra. Unleashing your divine potential of the word in this incarnation. It locks it fully into your heart chakra.

Sit in prayer position and repeat.

"I ask for the fifth key of Enock to unlock my throat chakra fully. And to lock away all issues that I have ever had with my throat chakra. I am that I am. And so it is. Amen."

The sixth key of Enock unlocks your third eye. Unlocks the divine potential within your visualizations. Unlocks the door to your mental body. Fully unleashing the power of your pineal gland and your visualizations within your merkaba. This is the most potent key for the realization of your manifestations upon the Earth plane within this incarnation. This key locks your third eye fully into your heart chakra and fully into your crown chakra and locks away any issues you have ever had with your manifestations in your visualizations. Unleashing the potential of your thought forms. Aligning you fully into the eye of Shiva. And locking the single eye. For when the Christ said "When the eye is single, the whole body shall be filled with light." It was this key he was referring to. As you unlock this, your body will be filled with light. Flooded with divine nectar.

Sit in prayer position and repeat.

"I ask that the sixth key of Enock unlocks my third eye completely. And locks away all issues that I have ever had with my third eye. I am that I am. And so it is. Amen."

The seventh key of Enock unlocks the Crown chakra fully. Unlocks all the divine gifts of the spirit. And anchors the four-body system fully into the Christ grid and into Mother Earth. In unlocking the crown chakra fully, the thousand-petal lotus opens and you walk into your Christhood. Fully emancipated. This locks the door to any and all entities that would try to interfere with you mission. This locks Satan up, not only for a thousand years but for the whole of your eternity. Free of the snares of the lower self. Locks away all issues that you have ever had with your crown chakra. Unlocks the resplendence of the Christ. Unlocks the detachment of the Buddha. Unlocks the full effulgence of spirit upon you. And the doves of peace descend upon you now.

Sit in prayer position and repeat.

"I ask that the seventh key of Enock unlocks my crown chakra fully. And locks away all issues I have ever had with my crown chakra. I am that I am. And so it is. Amen."

We ask that you repeat these statements every day for the first week of the twenty-one day period. You are ready to fully lock in your mission. Fully walk into your mastery.

Anchoring the light on a deeper, more energetic level will help you greatly. Allow this energy to sink into your consciousness. As you move forward every day on your twenty-one day transformation you will feel yourself becoming lighter and lighter as you drop the effects of negativity and all the issues that you have had within this lifetime. This is the initial freeing of energy lifting you. Breaking free of the shell of negativity that has been in this lifetime. Locking in all the positivity, so it will always be with you and locking away all the negativity so that it cannot harm you. And unlocking the effects of your divine potential will make your divine mission flow much easier. The first week we work on all of your issues within this incarnation. Anchoring you into your physical existence in this lifetime. You will feel freed very quickly and this will keep lifting you throughout the week until day eight when we will begin to work on your cosmic energy and the transformation initiations that will take you into your divine mastery fully in order to be nourished by the divine nectar. Fully freed from the Earth. Fully reliant on only God. Fully in your Christ self. This will affect you anyway but the more seriously you take this in your intent the quicker will be your transition. For faith has been described as belief, hope in the things that are unseen. But faith is the key to all things when you unlock your divine potential. With your thoughts you make the world. And on day twenty-one you will be called to make the leap of faith that will transcend all realities and bring you into pure divine enlightenment and oneness with all that is in order for you to be fully emancipated. And write your name in the book of life. Many are called. But you have been chosen. If you had not been chosen you would not be reading this text. Understand this. This is a divine text. You are chosen because of your past service and this is your reward.

The Lion of Judah is risen and is ready to roar. The keys of David are being given to unlock the Kingdom of God and to lock all those who would interfere with the manifestation of the Kingdom of God upon the Earth. As you unlock yourselves dear ones you pass the ring pass not. Clear your consciousness ready and allow yourself to be made fit for the down pouring of the Holy Spirit, the Holy grace of God until you become the walking Kingdom of God on the Earth plane. First unlock yourselves, and then allow the Holy Spirit to lock away all negativity around you. No earthly Jailer can unlock these locks and no earthly Jailer can lock them. These keys are the divine dispensation given to those who have proven themselves fit and worthy. The grace of God is upon you. The Lion shall lie down with the Lamb. For the two are the one and the same. The Lamb who sacrificed all. Ready for the wedding feast - which is now upon you. The Clarion Call has sounded. Many are called but few are chosen for this work. You are chosen or you would not be reading this. There is nothing ever to fear for I am with you. I am that which was here before I was born. I am in all Human hearts. Split a log and you will find me. Lift a rock and I am there. I am the Alpha and the Omega. The harvest is upon you. That which has been sown is ready to be reaped. The wheat shall be separated from the chaff and all will be burned up in the flame that I have given you.

Upon the eighth day of your twenty-one day transformation you are being given the key to the portal of Orion. This key is accessed through the pyramid in Giza. But it is a multi-dimensional portal. So it does not matter where you are upon the Earth plane for this to be effective. This key is the shape of the divine Ankh and is accessed through your heart chakra. This is a key to the tree of life and was originally used in divine ritual.

The sculpture you now call the sphinx. This grand sculpture originally had the head of a Lion. Which was changed to accommodate the ego of the Pharaoh. The divine order of Melchizedek, which ordained Yeshua and anointed the Holy ones ready for the divine mission within this batch of evolution, originally had their temples here. The Sphinx, sculpture of the Lion is the seventh of its kind that has been in this place on the Earth plane. When ultimately the desolation happens again all will be reset and a Golden Lion shall take its place. This event will not happen for thousands of years in your linear time. But it is important for you to understand what this sculpture was originally and that it represents the Lionheart, the Lion of Judah and in this current batch of evolution the root of David - the ordination and initiation of Melchizedek. The King of Kings and Lord of Lords of all things is indestructible within your aura now as you unlock your hearts with this key. You are a divine priest forever in the order of Melchizedek. The Holy Spirit and the doves of peace are upon you now.

As you progress through this cleanse every day taking the appropriate action and surrendering yourself to the divine will you will come fully into the zero point. Every action will become Holy. Every thought will become pure. Time will seem to stand still in these moments. Allow yourself to transform. Give no resistance to the process that is happening and all will become profoundly apparent as to what steps you need to take. You are being freed in the most profound of ways. And in anchoring yourself fully into the mission of the Christ you are being freed completely to create as you see fit. Once you pass the ring pass not.

We give you the breath of life initiation –

Sit in prayer pose.

Take a deep breath and hold it at the top.

We are anchoring your breath into your crown chakra.

As you breathe out feel all the energy going from your crown chakra to your base chakra.

Breathe out all the air. Hold at the bottom.

When you cannot hold any longer breathe in a full breath.

Hold at the top at your crown chakra.

When you cannot hold any more breathe out fully all the air in your lungs to the bottom.

When you cannot hold any more breathe in right to the top.

When you cannot hold any more breathe out all the air in your lungs.

When you cannot hold any more breathe in to the top of your lungs.

When you cannot hold any more breathe out and return to normal breath.

Feel the energy of the Christ heart opening up within you.

Do this three times a day from now on until you reach day twenty-one.

Your breath is very important in this process.

This divine template and this divine prophecy is being fulfilled because what has been projected from the past has embedded deeply into your consciousness. Each different batch of evolution of mankind has had a different Messiah, a different divine template, and a different divine story. Different points of fulfillment that had to be honored for the awakening, enlightenment and full transformation, transcendence and ascension of mankind. The words spoken in these books are tailor made. They are the key that fits the lock. For all the Saints and all the Martyrs, all the ascended souls that have helped over the last few millennia. To awaken and uplift you to the point where you are ready to transcend all things. Those who make it to this point in the book are ready to unlock themselves fully. Are ready to feel the effects of this divine prophecy fulfilled and the Christ consciousness to be anchored upon the Earth.

The next key we give you is the key of Hades. It is the key within your consciousness to lock Satan up for a thousand years. This is a symbolic time frame and what this means is complete annihilation of your lower selves and complete transcendence into your ascended vessel.

Sit in prayer pose and repeat the statement.

"I am that I am. I fully lock Satan away with the key of Hades. My lower self is locked away for all eternity. I am that I am. And so it is. Amen."

As you use this key of David within your consciousness the Earth plane become a transcended ascended place. And you are ready for the next stage of your divine plan to open up. All of these keys of your consciousness are very important and each one of them serves a different divine purpose.

As you arrive at day eight your journey with the Holy Spirit will intensify. You will have a feeling of lightness of being as you are shedding all the density from the Earth plane with the keys of the Kingdom and your acceptance of your Holy divine mission upon Earth at this time. This Holy mission is one of fun and laughter, transcendent bliss, purity and peace, chasing your highest excitement at all times and being led by your Spirit. Being shown the Golden path by the Holy Spirit. And as you recognize that the 'all that is' has your back. Is supporting you in all different ways you will move more and more into your divine confidence.

Day nine things will change again, becoming deeper and deeper. And from day nine you must daily reaffirm the first initiation from the trinity of Sai Baba's incarnation.

As you expand your awareness from day nine onwards it will become easier and easier as the power of a billion suns clears your pineal gland more and more and you visualize the divine nectar flowing into your palate. This is already happening simultaneously. Within your multi-dimensional energy system you are already surviving on prana. It is only the way that you are assimilating it that is changing dear ones. The clunky, clumsy way of assimilating food of an animal vibration into your vessel had its place at a certain level of consciousness. However as you transcend the different levels of vibration and you lift yourselves up this can no longer sustain you without you devolving greatly into great lessons of duality and pain, confusion and mental fog surrounding you, unhappiness and dis-ease. For the more you bring your vessel into a place of purity and heightened vibration the more it affects you when you lower your vibration once again. When you are in complete mastery of your four-body system and you are embodying the Christ you can imbibe anything and it will not have any effect upon your system. But you will have ultimate discernment and complete compassion so you would never indulge in such a thing. We only say this to make you aware of the vibration of complete purity that can transcend all things, that feels all things and that loves all things. And you can reach this level of purity very quickly when you transcend all things and ascend with your merkaba.

Day ten, day eleven, day twelve brings a deeper anchoring into the Christ grid. Every day from day ten you should do the divine meditation, the Christ grid twice a day, every day till day twenty one.

Day thirteen brings you to the next point of your heart mastery and your transcendent joy. Connecting with all beings that are going through and have gone through this process. Thirteen is the esoteric number of divine purity and is significant on many different levels - As the Christ in the centre surrounded by twelve disciples. As the divine vessel - going through the twelve stages throughout the year. Thirteen lunar stages. The esoteric stages of the divine Feminine. It has the numerical value of four, which is eleven-eleven, the divine twin flame. The point where the Yin and the Yang connect together and you are complete with your twin soul either in physical incarnation on the Earth plane or divine connection within the Yin Yang in spirit as the point in the centre. And the deeper embodiment of the peace that passes understanding. Complete anchoring into your consciousness of the thirteen muses of the Pleiades - the sisters of all encompassing mercy, joy and inspiration. From this day forward your multi-dimensional self will expand greatly. And you will be called to visualize the divine nectar dripping from your palate more and more. As often as you can from now on in.

Day fourteen brings you the deeper full anchoring of the five trees of paradise into your multi-dimensional self. As all the dedications from this book become fully flowered within your consciousness and you walk the path of Melchizedeks labyrinth. The double turning of seven - making fourteen within your consciousness. As you move forward through this day, Melchizidek and the Annunaki open up all physical synapses within your brain in your physical incarnation. Allowing the full awakening and understanding of the divine Kabbalah within your consciousness. As you are two thirds into the process being complete, this is a divine turning point and the expansion of your four-body system. Where the Kingdom within becomes the Kingdom without. And you prostrate yourself as a divine sacrifice in all that you say and all that you do for all of

Creation. You have already prepared yourself for this earlier in the book. This is the final anchoring of your divine commitment to all the statements that you have made. Cementing your divine intent within this incarnation - ready to make the leap of faith from your Earthly self into the full effulgence of your divine expression.

Day fifteen is a day of silence. You must prepare for this day beforehand as you move forward in this process. You may still communicate but we suggest a pen and a bit of paper for this day as it is a day of divine assimilation of all that has happened within this whole book and in the previous days of this process. This day of divine silence is very important for this process. If you are spending this day in your group of three, group of seven or beyond, it will be one of the most powerful group meditations that you have ever encountered. Be ready for divine epiphany and revelation and your column of white light being made stronger. If on this day you bi-locate to your ship of light for the first time, you will be intuitively led to all of the controls that you need to familiarize yourself with. If in this time there are other beings aboard the ship or if you have bi-located to one of the Mother ships, communicate energetically and telepathically. Do not say anything for this whole day no matter where your spirit leads you. If on this day it is the first day that you experience the divine nectar flowing, we suggest you spend your time in lotus or near lotus depending upon how flexible you are, with an upright spine as much as possible. And just spend the day letting the nectar flow. If this happens on this day, you will be in so much bliss; you will not be able to do anything else anyway.

Day sixteen is the divine day of the Merkaba. Go through all of the meditations from the Clarion Call on this day. If you have fully followed all instructions with discipline, to the letter, on this day you will feel a lightness of being that you have never experienced before and some of you may even levitate. If this happens to you on day sixteen, we suggest you spend the rest of the day in silence. Getting used to being able to levitate. Embracing your new found lightness. As your divine lightbody at this stage is completely transparent for those with eyes to see and your vocal expression constantly initiatic for those with ears to hear.

Day seventeen is the day of infinity, where all the Akashic records open up fully within your consciousness. And you are able to read the divine history of Gaia, completely if you so choose. It is giving you access to all your soul history. To all the soul extensions you have embodied all the way back to the Godhead within the gift of the linear expression of time - Gods greatest gift of illusion. From this point onward, you will have greater mastery over the linear expression of time and whilst in the zero point with a fully open Merkaba, you can express your preferences more lucidly within your Merkaba.

Day nineteen, day twenty and day twenty-one are days of divine assimilation, silence and expansion, days of complete transcendence, awareness and transformation. Within this silence you will have tasters of many other different forms of divine nectar from the higher dimensions, all the way through the many different levels towards source. There will be points of divine lightning and clearing your third eye and your pineal gland. You will feel this experience as fork lightning and sheet lightning. And you will become one with the divine nectar.

The Amarthans are offering their assistance with all the new processes that you are making. They are very excited to see you ascend and they look forward to a time when all your species are past the ring pass not and you can share the Earth together peacefully. Many of you will go through the twenty-one day process several times before you fully master it. And many of you will be fully fuelling and living on light the first time you have gone through the process. Some will not even have to do the twenty-one day process and the full visualization from the first initiation may bring the divine nectar into physical manifestation in your palate. No matter what stage you are at, how much effort you have put in to your mastery, to getting the hang of this process, to you transcending all things. The Amarthans wish to help you. They have a slightly different process in their physical vessels but they do experience divine nectar. The process of their opening happened a very long time ago but their cellular memory still holds the understanding of how it felt when they discovered they could live on light. Connecting with them in your merkaba. Connecting to the

North and the South Poles, visualizing the Earth as your vessel will connect you into their consciousness. They will give you visions through your third eye of what happened with their species before they all fully assimilated the process and ascended completely as a species. Many of them did not make it and they are still going through the process on other planets. As will many of your species. They will share with you the feelings they had. The cognitive dissonance they experienced and the feelings of elation and accomplishment as they were able to help their species one at a time as they discovered this divine gift. It is important to them that you understand the hand of friendship they are offering you, as they are eager and willing to give you their time. They send you great love at this time and will help you in this transition with individual glimpses of their crafts all over the world. We encourage this connection. We encourage this friendship and many of the other batches of humanity who have already transcended, ascended and completed the process are friends with many of the Amarthans. Those who are and have made this transition before also wish to help. There are less Humans here now than there are Amarthans but you may still connect with them if you have done the download implant from the first book for the intergalactic version of facebook. The whole of the Galactic Council now, every different species involved are lending their time and energy to your species at this time. Many different expressions of consciousness wish to connect. Those of you who love your canines, your Dogs, are encouraged to connect in with the many species of Canine that have evolved throughout the universe that are a part of the Galactic Council as are those who love Cats. Most of the wildlife upon your Earth has the evolved equivalent somewhere in the physical universe and if not in one of the multiverses. There is an evolved counterpart and alternate reality of anything you can imagine, for now it is important that you connect to the species that you relate to and resonate with most on a heart level. We appreciate that the majority of this expression is with your Cats and with your Dogs and therefore we encourage this greatly.

The expansion of your multi-dimensional selves at this new and expanded level of your consciousness in your linear time frame will speed up the ascension of your species, magnify the polarity, expand the conflict and help you transcend all antagonism to the expansion of your light. You are becoming fully active, non-reactive beings. We will give you a new download now to help with this process of full action within your new experience. **Non-reaction to outside circumstances.** It will help with your observation and your awareness.

Come into prayer pose.

Open to accept this download.

Feel it anchoring into your mental body.

Once you have fully assimilated this download it will help you see with more clarity the buttons that have been pushed by the many different beings you have encountered within this incarnation to make you react deliberately, to manipulate you in every different way.

Do not be afraid of your power dear ones. Do not be afraid of your divinity. We understand the waves of ascension can be very overwhelming. But the more and more you open up and accept your divinity, accept your power and accept your gifts, the more you will be helping all those who really need your help right now. Who really need your peace, who really need your calm, who really need your expanded mental body, who really need your expanded heart chakras, and who really need the inspiration of your divine nectar flowing. For although this is a transition in consciousness this is a very real divine battle and experience in humanity. The only weapon you ever need is your open Merkaba.

The more seriously you take your expansion, your gifts opening up and the power of your Merkaba, the quicker your transition will be. The more in bliss you will be and the more bliss you will experience on a day-to-day level, which will feed your Merkaba more and more. Which will be a wonderful transforming cycle leading to perpetual motion, intuitive living, ultimate bliss, joy, happiness and creation. And you will be so busy being in the flow of your own creativity that you will have no thought of fear, as you will see through the illusion in all its aspects.

The many different religions and philosophies on the Earth have many fervent supporters and dogmatic followers. And although many of them are indoctrinated and manipulated, the majority that believes in a philosophy are open hearted and kind individuals who only wish the best for mankind. And they can see no further than their own understanding. No matter which point of philosophy, you can learn from each and every one of them that embraces their faith or philosophy with single minded, pure and unadulterated focus. For each one of these processes manifests on the Earth plane through each of their divine intent. And they mistakenly believe that it is because of the validity of their individual faith instead of recognizing that it is because of the purity of their intent and beautiful devotion to their understanding that is manifest through their own divine God self. This is an important point for you to ponder. We do not negate any of your spiritual traditions; we actively encourage them until you are at the point of transcendence. Ready to walk into your full autonomy, ready to connect into your source, embodying that which you have felt led to worship. This worship had its place and has its place and is valid. The more you assimilate, read and embody every different concept we have given you, the more expanded your light body is going to become. And the more at ease you will be to embrace your divine self and start to play with the universe, opening your super consciousness fully. Transcending all ideas of right and wrong, up and down, hot and cold, dark and light, love and hate. For you *are* that divinity. And the final key of David we give you unlocks this reality within you and gives you authority and autonomy over all systems that are limiting in their nature as far as your expanding consciousness is concerned.

As you use this key all patterns of lack. Lack of bliss, lack of money, lack of friendship, lack of hope, lack of fun, lack of freedom, lack, lack, lack, shall dissolve. The concept of lack shall be locked away so that all that is left is the oneness.

You are encouraged to come here daily with your key.

You will see a door in front of you in your third eye.

Go through the motions of unlocking it.

Let the energy and intensity of this key assimilate into your consciousness before we move on.

The Arcturians – Are helping you transform the many levels of your light bodies. They are offering you an expansion download implant that will help with those of you who are working with extra terrestrials who have not passed the ring pass not. And who are trying to oppress the whole of your species in many different forms. The Arcturians are masters of light and are helping with your ascension and they are very well aware of the drama that is going on that has been instigated and perpetuated by many Lizard species that are having a negative impact upon your Earth plane. The different family dynasties that have a negative intent on the Earth plane and are trying to influence the policies of the Laws that are being designed to oppress you have no compassion in their make up. Believing their elite nature is one of privilege that cannot be overcome. However the Arcturians technology of light body transformation has made great strides in this area to help these species evolve. The recently ascended members of the Galactic Council and several of the planets in two different dimensions have noticed a knock on effect that happened with similar species that were trying to oppress their planets. Using this Arcturian technology on species that were in the process of oppressing which had a knock on effect on their species, helping to release the grip of oppression they had and in some cases even helped the Lizard population to transform and ascend prematurely.

We encourage you to play with this technology because what is happening on the Earth plane right now is on one level a great catalyst to bring you as a species to the next level of your ascension. But could also be used as a tool to help instill compassion into these Lizard extra terrestrials. We encourage you to assimilate this into your consciousness and play with the technology with the ones you understand are of a lizard lineage.

Those of you who would like to take advantage of this offer from the Arcturians come into prayer pose.

Accept this download.

This was a last minute interjection by the Arcturians who asked to participate in this book. They are happy to gift you this download. When you use this download and you are seeing a situation that needs help on the Earth plane. You can visualize this as a sword of light. You activate this sword of light with your intent. It is affective against any of the Lizard population - If not to bring them into compassion - to at least subdue their intention in the moment. Depending on the strength and level of your intent, your prayer, your divine resonance and your mastery over your merkaba. You can strengthen this wand of light, this sword technology, to the point where you can turn things around for these species. This has effectively become a double ascension on the Earth plane with this interjection by the Arcturians. Your visualizations in this regard are greatly appreciated by them.

ArchAngel Michael – Wishes to activate fully your sword of divine truth. This blue sword is already upon your four-body system. All you need do is activate it. In order to activate it all you need do is hold your heart with your hand and pull the sword from your heart chakra. Pull it from your heart as if your heart is the scabbard encasing it. This blue saber light effectively gives you the power of Michael. At this point you embody ArchAngel Michael. You become a divine conduit of truth. Wielding the sword of truth wherever you go. It is a mighty and powerful tool for you to activate. You will greatly benefit from this once you have - cutting away all falsehood. Affording you divine protection.

The twenty-four elders – Are activating the flaming swords of divine truth, the golden swords of fire and divine protection. These are surrounding you now from all directions - Twenty-four swords of flaming, golden divine protection. Expanding from all directions. Nothing can penetrate these swords. They are the swords that surround the throne. They are being activated within you now. All you need do is be aware of them. You will see this process through your third eye. **This activation is spontaneous and compulsory once you get to this stage in the book**. For you are moving into territory that no human within your batch of evolution moved forward through in your linear time frame before the turn of your century. It is only members of the 144,000 that have volunteered their soul expression to expand in this way that will be reading these words. All trivialities will lessen and lessen as you move forward past this point in the book. It is a very important point of the ring-pass-not. A different, more divine stage of the ring-pass-not that you are ready for because you are reading these words. This divine fire of the Elohim is the most purifying thing that you can experience within your consciousness at this level of your evolution. All who are reading these words will be transformed on a moment-to-moment basis through this divine fire from this moment onwards. This is the highest level of divine fire that you can experience. The only thing that can stop this now is a special dispensation from the almighty source. If you work with this consciously only upon your own consciousness the divine mirror of your experience will transform the more that you allow it to transform you.

All that has been happening. Every different moment within your experience has been leading you towards your mission, towards the emancipation of your own consciousness, the consciousness of those around you and the whole of mankind. We ask you to look towards the synchronicities, the coincidences, and the seemingly inconsequential connections. For every connection is relevant dear ones. Every different connection is relevant to the point of consciousness that you are resonating with in the moment.

With consciousness always vacillating between higher and lower density, higher and lower vibration, as you move forward towards your mastery. The vibration you are exhibiting, expressing and that is beaming from your essence in any given moment is the catalyst for the message that you receive from the universe. When you are in a lower, argumentative, depressed state of being, you see messages from the universe that reinforces this vibration. And when you raise your vibration to the point of bliss, all the synchronicities are from that higher point of vibration. This is why we recommend you coming into bliss. Actively seeking it. Using different ways to expand your bliss. Breathing properly, eating properly, thinking properly. Properly is all relative for everything is an experience of God, even depression, pain, and heartache. There is no such thing as a negative in reality for all is an expression of the one, an expression of divine experience. But as you ascend more and more your experiences of bliss become more and more consistent as you recognize that you have an option, you have a say in how you are feeling, how you are reacting to any given thing and how you are acting in any given moment. The more you recognize this the more you will act upon this. The more you act upon this, the more bliss you will bring in. You will recognize all the things that work within your consciousness. When we urge you to stay away from artificial stimulants it is not because you do not enjoy these in the moment. It is because of the boomerang effect of these things for anything that brings you so high on an artificial level will also bring you low when you have come out of this vibration, which will cause confusion within your vessel. Therefore we encourage highs that are of a natural origin. Your endorphins do not have a low equivalent. Your tantric bliss does not have a low equivalent. Your Yogic bliss does not have a low equivalent. Your meditational bliss does not have a low equivalent. These are things that bind together in order to bring you to your state of mastery for mastery in this sense is recognizing that you have a choice. Recognizing that you are deciding to feel negative or positive within any given moment. And when you understand the tools that you have to bring yourself into a higher vibration. Concentrating on your breath, doing yoga, exercising, alkalizing your body, drinking water, concentrating on your love essence, concentrating on your heart chakras, concentrating on breathing into your merkaba, into the flower of life, into opening up all these wonderful tools for the transformation of your consciousness into bliss. You will choose nothing else, why would you. And once you realize it is a choice in any given moment you can act upon the choice that will bring you into a higher state of being. All the downloads, the upgrades, the meditations, initiations, everything that we give you is to bring you into that higher point of vibration in order for you to open up the divine nectar that will flow through your palate. So you are focused and balanced in your equanimity. From this place of balance you help everyone else come into their balance. Just naturally staying in your high vibration helps everyone around you, helps the whole world. Your mission is always within your own vibration, within your own bliss, within your own balance. The more you open up to this, the more you embody the one energy, the more you embody God, the more you recognize yourself as the witness of all things.

In order to bring you deeper into your bliss we recommend **ten breaths, ten times a day - Of a deep nature.**

You can always afford to be alone for ten breaths dear ones. Even if you visit the toilet, allow yourselves to be alone for ten breaths. With these ten breaths, open yourself up, open your lungs up, right to the top and then breathe out.

Slow and deep as you breathe in feel yourself anchoring into the centre of the Earth and your crown chakra anchoring into the Christ grid.

Every breath centering in on your heart chakra.

By the third breath we ask you to repeat the mantra within your head.

"Thank you for all that has been. Thank you for all that is. And thank you for all that is to come."

As you repeat this in your mind, with your breath, you activate your abundance within all parts of your life.

"Thank you for all that has been. Thank you for all that is. And thank you for all that is to come."

This is the abundance mantra. It will magnify the abundance romantically, financially, physically, and emotionally. All different areas will be considered and will be magnified in the positive.

"Thank you for all that has been. Thank you for all that is. And thank you for all that is to come."

In coming into the divine flow of your gratitude for all that you have experienced in this incarnation. All the experiences, all the highs and lows as you perceive it. As you send out gratitude the universe responds by magnifying your pleasure, magnifying your abundance – magnifying your blessings. For this life is a blessing dear ones and as you are reading this book you are being blessed, you are being transformed. These ten breaths, ten times a day will help in this transformation.

All the words that we have expressed in this book and book one, the healing book and the Clarion call are all you need to dive into the very depth of your being, the very depth of your Christ light. Emancipating your consciousness wholly and completely. All the different codes, all the different characters, all the different embodiments of God are different within each divine drama of the emancipation of a species.

The masters of light, when you walk your Earth plane now, are encoded with all your divine stories, ready to emancipate your consciousness, fully into the oneness. These multi-dimensional kickers are the most potent that there has ever been within your batch of evolution. And as you have gotten to this point in the book you are being encoded with everything that you need in order to fully emancipate those who come into contact with you. Do not take these words lightly, for they are very potent. And just the fact that you are reading at this stage in the book means that reading the text has already changed you. You are emancipated, you have risen, and you are ready.

The Annunaki are encoding all the codes of light upon you now in your mental body. Expanding your mental awareness once again as you are ready to come into the next level of your expansion and transformation.

Come into prayer pose.

Allow this expansion of your mental body.

The Annunaki are encompassing your whole vessel now.

Transforming your mental mastery.

Expanding your super-conscousness.

Fully activating all the dormant parts of your D,N,A that have not yet been fully anchored.

The waves of mental stimulation and the firing of your synapses are upgrading your mental body in the deepest way that is possible be upgraded within a human vessel now.

Allow this mental upgrade to fully embed. This will help you fully assimilate all of the mental kickers within this book that have had to be read first before you could receive this final gift from the Annunaki. They are happy to see you come to this point in your expansion and are eager to help you. You may call upon them at any time. They will connect with you with sound codes as you fully expand into this upgrade. **Each time you do ten breaths, ten times a day, you will be fully anchoring this mental upgrade**. Symbolically, they wash your feet once again. They thank you for your service. They look forward to your connection together.

Once you have made the transition and the divine nectar starts to flow you will never look back. Your life will become a symphony where once it was a whistled tune. It will become a novel where once it was a pamphlet. It will become a delight and a blessing to all that connect with you. Your divine powers will open up. More and more your manifestations will become instant. You will get the hang of how to manifest out of thin air, how to access the different dimensions, how to come into the zero point and freeze time within your experience as you fuel your merkaba with your divine nectar. For this Amrita is so beautiful in its taste, even the experience of it opens your heart and the more your heart opens the more love you flow with, the more love you flow with the easier it is to fuel your merkaba. Your clairaudience, your clairvoyance, your clairsentience, your clairgustience, all of your psychic senses will open up fully. Your connection into the Akashic records will be complete. And you will have a buoyancy, a lightness of being that you have never felt before.

We are delighted you have reached this stage in your evolution and you are ready for the final initiation.

Stand with your feet slightly apart.

Put your hands on your heart.

The Lord Jesus Christ stands in front of you.

His hands on your shoulders.

He embraces you now.

Pulling you into his heart.

You are being baptized and transformed in the name of the Father and the Sun and the Holy Spirit.

You are becoming one.

You are surrounded by Prema Sai, Sathya Sai and Shirdi Sai Baba. They surround you now.

You are one with Christ.

The whole of the heavenly hierarchy surrounds you now. All of the Galactic Council surrounds you in a massive circle of the flower of life.

All the divine light from all of the divine beings past the ring-past-not, up to and including the Godhead are surrounding you now.

You are being infused with divine light. The divine manna of God is now flowing through you and your pineal gland is fully activated.

You are bi-located simultaneously to the centre of all the suns in all the multiverse.

All the power that ever was, ever is and ever will be is yours now.

All the seals are open!

You are unlocked fully to the furthest point you can go in this incarnation in a human vessel.

All the divine blessings are upon you now.

Repeat the statement.

"I am that I am. And so it is. Amen."

This final initiation brings you fully into your divine self and welcomes you into your experience in the golden age of mankind. Allow yourself to embrace this, as the full immensity will come upon you in waves, expanding and expanding your divine purity. For every second from now on your vibration will build upon this positive and your awareness of your expansion will expand more and more. You are a fully Christed being with full membership to the Galactic Council. Your acceptance of this will expand more and more as you are empowered in all ways within your four-body system, within your awareness, in your powers of speech and vibrational influence. You are a lighthouse; here to shine the light and embody your bliss, embody your purity. There is no more going back. All your gifts shall open up. You are now free. Fully supported and protected by the heavenly hierarchy. We thank you for your service. As your bliss expands and you are led at all times by your highest excitement, your divine intuition, the golden compass of your heart, embodying the peace that passes understanding - All that need your light will be drawn to you. You have much to do - you have many blessings to give. And the expansion of your heart from this point onward will forever multiply. Your whole body is filled with light.

All the seals are now open. All prophecy is fulfilled in divine righteousness. Those who have ears will hear. Those who have eyes will see.

Those who are transformed will understand.

There is nothing more to do but be still and embody your divinity.

The time has come.

Printed in Great Britain
by Amazon

45429696R00040